Inside the Mind of
A FIERCE LION

ANIMAL INSTINCTS

TOM JACKSON

PowerKiDS press

New York

Published in 2012 by The Rosen Publishing Group, Inc.
29 East 21st Street, New York, NY 10010

Editor: Julia Adams
U.S. Editor: Julia Quinlan
Book Design: Paul Cherrill

Photo Credits: All images and graphic elements by Shutterstock, apart from: p. 8 (inset): Paul Souders/Corbis; p. 11 (all insets): iStock; p. 12 (inset): STR/Reuters/Corbis; pp. 12/13: Martin Harvey/Alamy; p. 1 and p. 14: Paul Souders/Corbis; p. 15 (bottom inset): Dreamstime; p. 16: Ross Warner/Alamy; p. 17 (top): Malcolm Schuyl/FLPA; p. 16 (bottom): David T. Grewcock/FLPA; p. 19 (top inset): Dreamstime; p. 21 (skull): Dave King/Getty Images; p. 22 (inset): Photos.com; p. 24: Mike Hill/Alamy; p. 25 (inset): Ace Stock Limited/Alamy; pp. 26/27: Steve Bloom Images/Alamy; p. 28: AFP/Getty Images; p. 29 (main image): Jon Hrusa/epa/Corbis.

Library of Congress Cataloging-in-Publication Data

Jackson, Tom, 1972–
  Inside the mind of a fierce lion / by Tom Jackson. — 1st ed.
      p. cm. — (Animal instincts)
  Includes index.
  ISBN 978-1-4488-7032-5 (library binding) — ISBN 978-1-4488-7074-5 (pbk.) — ISBN 978-1-4488-7075-2 (6-pack)
  1. Lion—Behavior—Juvenile literature. I. Title.
  QL737.C23J333 2012
  599.75'515—dc23

                    2011028821

Manufactured in the United States of America

CPSIA Compliance Information: Batch #WW2102PK: For Further Information contact Rosen Publishing, New York, New York at 1-800-237-9932

CONTENTS

Mighty Lions

Are you scared of lions? You probably should be. Attacks are very rare—lions don't usually hunt for people—but these big cats are one of the world's top **predators**.

The lion is the biggest cat living in **Africa**. It is also the noisiest, with its loud roars. Only lions and other "big cats" can roar. Smaller ones, like house cats, do not have the right voice box. They can only snarl and purr.

LION FACT FILE

Height:
male: 4 ft (1.2 m);
female: 3.6 ft (1.1 m)

Length:
male: 7.9 ft (2.4 m);
female: 6 ft (1.8m)

Weight:
male: 530 lbs (240 kg);
female: 353 lbs (160kg)

Average human:
height: 5.5 ft (1.7 m);
weight: 155 lbs (70 kg)

Fangs can rip through meat.

Padded paws mean lions can creep up on prey.

Mother lions keep their cubs hidden and move them to different dens every few days. This is so predators will not sniff them out.

Lionesses lift their cubs by the skin on the back of their neck while they can't walk. It doesn't hurt them.

When cubs begin walking, they follow their moms.

WOW!

A lion cub weighs 3.3 pounds (1.5 kg) when it is born. That is about half the size of a human baby.

A cub can walk when it is 15 days old.

Joining the Gang

Lions are the only cats that live in a family group, called a **pride**. When the cubs are two months old, their mom brings them to the pride for the first time.

All of the cubs in a pride play together. They pretend to hunt and play fight with each other.

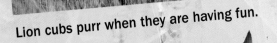

Lion cubs purr when they are having fun.

Cubs do not meet their fathers until they are old enough to join the pride.

Prides stick together. They play, rest, and hunt together. Prides even clean each other! Lionesses will lick their cubs until they are clean.

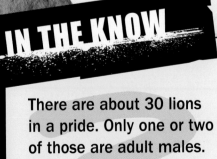

As male cubs grow up, the leader of the pride starts seeing them as a threat.

A lion's rough tongue combs out dirt and bugs.

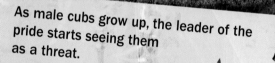

IN THE KNOW

There are about 30 lions in a pride. Only one or two of those are adult males. They are very protective, so they won't let other males come close to the pride.

Food for the Pride

The adult females provide the pride with food. The lionesses work as a team to kill animals that are too large for one lion to kill on its own. The male rarely helps, but males that don't live in a pride have to hunt on their own.

Cubs do not hunt with their mothers. They hide in tall grasses and watch.

Cubs eat their first meat at about three months old. They continue drinking milk for a few more months. They can get milk from any lioness in the pride, not just their mother.

Lionesses take turns looking after the cubs while the other lionesses hunt.

The lionesses make sure the buffalo herd can see them.

But one lioness sneaks off to the other side of the herd…

They charge!

The buffalo is trapped! The lionesses take turns attacking.

Meet the Neighbors

A lion pride has a **territory**, a home area just for them. The male defends it against lions from other prides. But there are plenty of other animals that pass through, whether the lions like it or not.

Many people like to go on safaris. These are trips through savannahs and other habitats. People can see lions when on a safari.

As long as lions don't feel threatened, they won't attack the tourists.

This large bird snatches lion cubs from their dens.

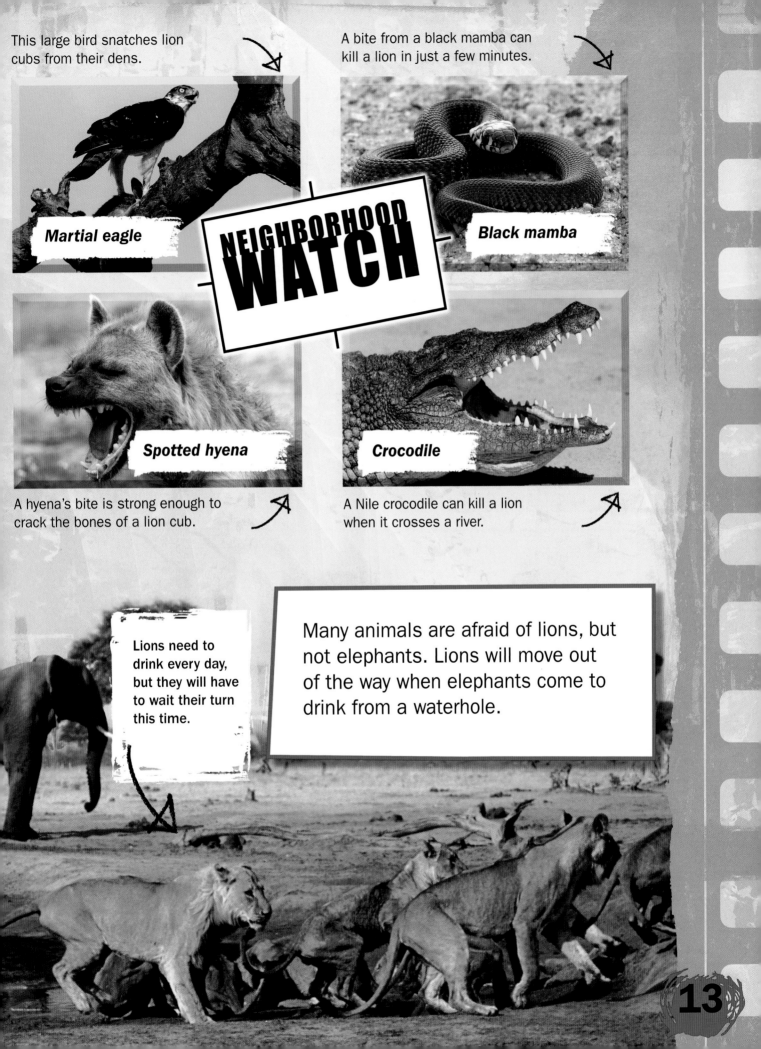

Martial eagle

A bite from a black mamba can kill a lion in just a few minutes.

Black mamba

NEIGHBORHOOD WATCH

Spotted hyena

A hyena's bite is strong enough to crack the bones of a lion cub.

Crocodile

A Nile crocodile can kill a lion when it crosses a river.

Lions need to drink every day, but they will have to wait their turn this time.

Many animals are afraid of lions, but not elephants. Lions will move out of the way when elephants come to drink from a waterhole.

13

Forced Out

When a male lion reaches about two years old, he will be forced to leave the pride by his father. This is before he grows strong enough to take over!

Once young lions have been forced out of the pride they grew up with, they must fend for themselves until they are strong enough to have their own pride.

WOW!

An adult male lion is 176 lbs (80 kg) heavier than a lioness and about three times as heavy as a man!

The mane begins to grow at the age of two. It will make the lion look even bigger and stronger.

Lions sharpen their claws by scraping them on trees.

Claw marks and sprays of **urine** on trees signal that a new lion is in the area.

Claw Action

Like all cats, lions keep their claws tucked into their paws, so they stay sharp. When the lion needs its claws, muscles flick each one into action.

When the lion's toes are relaxed, its claws are tucked in.

When it attacks, the lion stretches its toes, and the claws slide out.

Sensors On

As lions grow up they become stronger and stronger. They learn to use their powerful senses to find food and tell their friends from their enemies.

Lions have a powerful sense of smell. They can smell other lions that are in the same area. They can even tell if a lion is a male or female, just from the way they smell.

A lion's ears can turn to hear where a sound is coming from.

Lions can pick up smells with the roof of their mouth.

Lions eyes sometimes look like they are glowing in the dark.

Lions have excellent night vision. This lets them hunt at night. They must be careful of other lions, though.

Shining Eyes

Lions' eyes reflect light. This is because lions have a special layer in their eyes. Reflecting the light helps them see better in the dark. When the light is reflected, it looks like the eyes are glowing. All cats have this special layer in their eyes, even domestic cats.

Hunting Alone

When a male lion hunts alone, most of his attacks fail. He can go for days without food, but if he doesn't get enough to eat he may never grow strong enough to become a pride leader.

It is difficult for male lions to hunt by themselves. They must hide and wait for vulnerable prey.

Lions can recognize each other by the pattern of spots on the snout.

The lion pounces on the wildebeest. His hook-shaped claws dig into its back.

The wildebeest cannot escape the lion's grip and is pulled to the ground.

One bite to the wildebeest's neck crushes the throat and kills it.

WOW!

A lion's mouth is big enough for a person's head to fit in!

Now the lion has to stand guard over his prey, so hyenas don't steal any of it.

Dinner Time

A lion always sits down for its meals. It eats most of its prey, except the stomach, brain, and bones.

Lions will eat the leftovers from another animal's kill. They prefer fresh meat, though. Lions start by eating the belly of their kill and end with the head.

Lions use their fangs to grip flesh and rip off chunks of it.

The lion's rough tongue is great for licking scraps of meat off bones.

Lions cannot eat a whole wildebeest at once. They need to rest before they can finish eating.

Lion Skull and Teeth

A lion's head is built for biting. The back half of the skull is covered in a huge muscle that pulls the jaw closed with great force. If the jaw gets injured, the lion cannot bite properly and the animal soon starves to death.

Small, sharp **incisors** can cut through skin and flesh

Large, strong **molars** grind food and even bones

Eye socket

Brain case

Canine teeth (or fangs) are used to kill prey

Height (open mouth): 10 in (25 cm)

Back teeth work like slicing scissors

Lower jaw

Length: 16 in (40 cm)

Taking a Rest

Lions eat a lot and eat very quickly. A big male can gobble up 66 lbs (30 kg) of food (the weight of a 10-year-old child) in about an hour. All that meat needs time to **digest**.

Away from the pride, male lions can eat as much as they want. That means they have to take extra time to rest and digest, though.

The skin on a lion's belly is folded so it can stretch to fit a stomach full of food.

WOW!

A lion sleeps for 20 hours after a big meal.

Lions may leave part of their kill for the next day, if they are too full to finish. Eating a lot helps make a lion strong.

Lions are very light sleepers and can spring awake and into action in a flash.

Ready to Fight

At about four or five years old, a male lion is ready to be pride leader. He can claim a territory and attract females from neighboring prides to join him. Or he can fight and beat another chief lion.

Once a lion has lived on his own for a while he becomes strong enough to have his own pride. To show that they are strong, male lions will roar loudly during the night.

A dark, thick mane is a sign that this male is very strong.

IN THE KNOW

Lions roar most at night when the air is still, so all the other lions in the area can hear them. You can hear a lion roaring 5 miles (8km) away!

Male lions try to attract lionesses from other prides.

Lions can smell when lionesses are ready to mate.

A lion's mane protects from bites and scratches in a fight.

Before the two lions can mate the male lion must fight the leader of the lioness's pride.

King of the Pride

When a young lion wins his fight, the old leader moves away. The young lion becomes head of the pride. This means he has to protect the pride from danger, such as other lions.

When a young lion takes over a pride, he will want to have cubs. To do this he must first get rid of the old pride leader's cubs.

When their cubs are being attacked, lionesses can be fierce – even towards a pride leader.

Male lions spend a lot of their time guarding and marking their pride's territory. Pride leaders want to protect their cubs, even though male cubs could grow to become threats.

The pride often moves to look for herds of animals it can attack for food.

IN THE KNOW

A new chief lion wants to have cubs as soon as possible, but the lionesses need to finish feeding their older cubs first. So the new male leader kills those cubs. This means that their mothers will be ready to mate with him a few days later.

Saving Lions

Africa's lions need to be protected because their numbers are going down. People who help protect animals are called **conservationists**. They work to make sure that lions will not die out.

The biggest threat to lions are humans. If a lion comes into a village, local people may shoot it, worried that it may attack them. Farmers also shoot lions to stop them killing their cattle. A lion cannot tell the difference between a farm animal and a wild one.

A farmer with a cow that has been killed by a lion.

Conservationists protect lions by moving them away from farms and villages. They first shoot each lion with a dart filled with sleeping drugs. The sleeping lion is put in a cage and moved to a safe area.

The sleeping drugs in the darts work after less than five minutes and put the lion to sleep for about two hours.

The best place to keep lions safe is in nature reserves. These are huge areas of land where farming is not allowed and very few people live. So the lions can live wild.

A fence stops lions from straying into dangerous areas.

29

QUIZ

1) Lions are like house cats. They spend most of their time alone. True or false?

2) Bones, legs, liver, eyeballs: Which one of these things do lions NOT eat?

3) Why do a lion's eyes appear to glow in the dark?

4) Can all types of cats roar?

5) Why are lion cubs born with marks?

6) Who does all the hunting for the pride?

7) How old are male lions when they start to grow a mane?

Answers:
1) Lions mostly live in groups, called prides. But young male lions sometimes live on their own. This is after they have left the pride they grew up in and before they take over as leader of a new pride.
2) Just bones – yes they eat the eyeballs too!
3) Because they have a layer in their eyes that reflects light.
4) No just big cats like lions, tigers, leopards, and jaguars.
5) To disguise them better in the grass.
6) The lionesses.
7) Two years.